GOLD RUSH!

The Yukon Stampede of
1898

MARGARET POYNTER

GOLD RUSH!

The Yukon Stampede of 1898

ILLUSTRATED WITH PHOTOGRAPHS & MAPS

Atheneum   1979   New York

Library of Congress Cataloging in Publication Data

Poynter, Margaret.   Gold rush!

SUMMARY: Recounts the Klondike gold rush of 1896–8
and both the greed and heroism of the people
inflamed with gold fever.

1. Klondike gold fields—Juvenile literature.
[1. Klondike gold fields.   2. Gold mines and mining]
I. Title.

F1095.K5P69   971.9′1   78–14503
ISBN 0–689–30694–6

TO MY MOTHER AND FATHER

*Through your eyes I have seen the land
of the sourdough;
Through your hearts I came to love it.*

Contents

ACKNOWLEDGMENTS

My thanks to Dodd, Mead and Company for their kind permission to use selections from the poetry of Robert Service.

And my special gratitude to Don Meyer, who reproduced my photographs with such tender loving care.

Preface

KLONDIKE! YUKON! ALASKA! GOLD! In 1898
these magical words had cast a spell over thousands
of people all over the world. The stampede into the
northern wilderness was in full force. In the United
States doctors left their waiting rooms full of patients. Railroad conductors left their passengers
stranded. Farm workers left grain to rot in the
fields.

A year earlier most of these people had never
even heard of the Klondike River or the Yukon Valley. To them Alaska had been just a shadowy, form-
less territory filled with Eskimos and polar bears.

But they had all heard of gold. They were willing to abandon their businesses and their jobs, sell
their homes, and leave their families to go in search
of the shiny yellow metal.

Their reasons were understandable. The
United States was in the midst of a severe depression. Many businesses were faltering. Men were
lucky to find just a few days of work now and then.

Thousands of homes were under threat of foreclosure, and children were going to bed hungry. Hopeless men and women decided that they had nothing to lose by taking their chances in the gold fields. They begged, borrowed, and sometimes stole for passage and supplies.

Their lives were drastically changed as a result of their participation in the stampede. There is no doubt, also, that the face and fortune of the gold country itself was changed. No longer would these northern outposts of civilization be unknown, uncharted wildernesses. Alaska suddenly became attractive to farsighted businessmen. Railroads were built in response to the demand for transportation. Telegraph lines were laid, and law and order came to the raw, bustling frontier. As in California, the gold rush brought Alaska many years closer to statehood.

The Great Stampede of '98 also brought forth its own brand of literature. One of the greatest of the gold rush poets was Robert W. Service. Service felt the pain and despair, the joy and the rewards, and the passion and insanity of gold fever. He was able to put these feelings into words and preserve them for future generations.

GOLD RUSH!

The Yukon Stampede of 1898

1

A Restless Race of Men

There's a race of men that don't fit in,
A race that can't stay still;
So they break the heart of kith and kin,
And they rove the world at will.
They range the field and they rove the flood,
And they climb the mountain's crest;
Theirs is the curse of the gypsy blood,
And they don't know how to rest.

THE MEN WHO DON'T FIT IN—*Service*

Fishing and fur trading—in the 1700s and the 1800s these two occupations gave the Indians of Alaska and western Canada everything they needed. They often noticed shiny flakes of gold along the shores of rivers, but to them the metal was of little value. The salmon in those streams represented their wealth.

3

White men also roamed the Indian country in those early days. Russians, Frenchmen, and employees of the British Hudson's Bay Company picked up nuggets from the beds of streams. They may have kept some of the larger ones as souvenirs. Most of them they threw back. To them also, the treasure of the North lay in the furs of the beaver, the marten, and the wolverine.

The inhabitants of this wild country had come to terms with the death-dealing weather and the lack of modern conveniences. On the whole, they were satisfied with their way of life and wanted no changes. There were, however, events occurring in the outside world which were slowly, but inevitably, leading to great upheavals in their lives.

The first such notable event was the discovery of gold in California in 1848. When these gold fields dwindled, prospectors began to work their way up toward the southern coast of Alaska. By the 1860s they were mining on the "Panhandle," the long strip of coastal land bordering on British Columbia. When the United States bought Alaska in 1867, the miners were joined by other Americans who felt the need to flee from civilization. Men who had sought for gold in South Africa and Australia also headed north to try their luck.

As strikes were made, the news leaked out and others came rushing to the area. Towns such as

Juneau and Sitka were established. Dance hall girls, saloon keepers, road agents, and gamblers arrived. One by one, and two by two, the prospectors left the sound of the honky-tonk piano and the saw mills and pushed on. They took with them only a rucksack, a gold pan, a short-handled shovel, and some beans, bacon, and tea.

They also took their crock of sourdough. Sourdough is a fermented dough mixture which is used with flour and water in place of yeast to make biscuits and flapjacks rise. Since a diet of beans alone was intolerable, to be without sourdough would have been flirting with starvation. Thus, these hardened pioneers came to be known as "sourdoughs" to separate them from the "cheechakos," or tenderfeet.

During the 1870s and 1880s the sourdoughs drifted into the Yukon Valley from three directions. George Holt was the first white man to slip past the three thousand Indian guards of the Chilkoot Pass. This pass was a small gap in the jagged southern mountain range. Holt managed to carry some gold nuggets back to Sitka. Though he was later killed by members of an inland Indian tribe, his death did not discourage others from following in his footsteps.

Ed Schieffelin went around the coast of the Bering Sea and up the Yukon River. Schieffelin's eyes had the dreamy, faraway look of the prospector. With his shabby clothes and his long black hair and beard, no one suspected that he was a millionaire. He had already founded the town of Tombstone, Arizona, and was looking for new challenges. After traveling a thousand miles into the interior, he decided that mining would never pay in the bleak countryside. He retraced his route and left the northland.

Arthur Harper was a tall, bearded Irishman with piercing eyes. He and his friends plodded and prospected along two thousand miles from the interior of Canada to the point where the Yukon crosses the Arctic Circle. He was to spend the next twenty-five years roaming up and down the river.

Other prospectors reached the Yukon Valley in steadily increasing numbers for the next few years. When the Chilkoot Indians found that the newcomers were not looking for furs, they felt less threatened by their presence. They went to work packing supplies over the pass for the white men. By 1886 two hundred gold seekers had crossed over this route.

The trading posts, which formerly had stocked supplies for only the natives and the fur traders, found it profitable to add mining equipment. Since the prospectors no longer had to return to the coast every spring to replenish their gear, they were now able to stay in the interior and prospect wider areas. New gold fields were discovered. The "moccasin telegraph" spread the news. Gradually, the trickle of newcomers into the valley changed into a small stream.

COMMUNITIES grew up around the trading posts, strikes increased, and small scale gold rushes started to occur. These rushes, no matter how small, were called "stampedes." The waves of excitement brought more people to the area. Towns were born, grew, and prospered. It often happened that before a year had passed, some of these towns had died, for the typical prospector was a restless man. He became bored shoveling dirt on the same old sandbar. News of a strike filled him with a yearning for new horizons and adventure. He willingly abandoned his cabin, left a claim which was paying a steady five dollars a day, and slogged across the country. He knew with a certainty that every step he took was bringing him closer to his "bonanza," or big strike.

If he didn't hit paydirt in the new field, his disappointment was fleeting. After all, he reflected, there would always be another stampede, another mountain to cross. It was the search, more than the gold itself, which was the important thing.

He treasured freedom from restraint and rules

and obligations. His time belonged to him. He marked it only by the breakup of the river ice in the spring and by the first flurry of snow in the fall. In between there was winter, when travel was difficult or impossible, and there was summer, when he could move easily from place to place.

In order to survive, he depended upon his own abilities and what the land had to offer. When he took to the river, he built a boat. When he stopped for the winter, he built a cabin. He shot moose and bear, and ate the meat and made clothes from the furs and skins. When he needed warmth, he gathered wood and built a fire.

Since he spent so much time by himself, he developed and retained his own unique personality. He was usually tagged with a nickname which set him apart. There was Salt Water Jack, Squaw Cameron, Pete the Pig, and Cannibal Ike. The latter got his name from eating hunks of raw moosemeat.

There was a ferocious looking character named Cutthroat Johnson. He didn't bother to tell anyone the only throat he had ever cut was his own. He wore a thick, tangled beard to cover the scar which had resulted from a drunken suicide attempt.

In spite of their individualism and their love of independence, these men were bound together in a loose brotherhood. They were expected to follow the rules of this brotherhood. These rules came to be known as the Yukon Code. Sourdoughs abided by this code, not only because they were supposed to, but because they had a real concern for each other. This concern was necessary in a land where a helping hand meant the difference between life and death.

Every cabin was left unlocked even if there was a hefty poke of gold inside of it. Anyone who needed shelter and food felt free to stay a night or two. On the other hand, he was obligated to clean up after himself, lay in a fresh stock of firewood, and replenish the food supply when he was able.

Most trading post operators followed the code by extending almost unlimited credit to someone who was down on his luck. If supplies were short, they were distributed equally regardless of whether a man could pay or not. It was agreed that no one should starve just because his claim hadn't paid off.

It was also agreed that in such a society, no man should have to steal, though murder, under certain circumstances, could be forgiven. Theft was punishable by hanging or by banishment from the territory.

According to the code, whenever a man made a strike, it was his duty to inform other prospectors in the area as soon as possible. In fact, the greatest joy in finding gold was the spreading of the news.

Any man who kept his discovery to himself was scorned and shunned by his fellow sourdoughs.

A SOURDOUGH could be a millionaire or a pauper; he could be a college graduate or have no formal education; he could be a skilled artisan or a laborer; he could be an American, a Russian or a German. He might spend his leisure hours playing cards and drinking, or he might discuss the fine points of Greek mythology with others who had similar interests.

They all had imagination and ingenuity. They would not have been able to survive the harsh winter without them. One tall tale tells of a man who had just shot a bear, but was still in danger of starving. He had lost all of his teeth from scurvy. In desperation, he made a set of dentures from his tin tableware and the bear's teeth.

"I et that bear with his own teeth," he later bragged to his friends.

Most sourdoughs were incurable gamblers. They won and lost their claims on the turn of a card. They bet on the exact time the ice would break up, on when the steamer would arrive, and on whether the next man who came in the trading post door would step in with his right foot or his left foot.

They had developed a fierce loyalty to the

Northland. To them it represented the last frontier. They expressed their pride and devotion to it in an abundance of stories, poems, and songs. They then read their own writing and believed every word of it.

At times this belief was the only thing that enabled men to endure the isolation, backbreaking labor, and the constant dangers. Just surviving in the Yukon was a continuing challenge. To stay enthusiastic and hopeful would have been impossible without the bonanza which was always just beyond the next river.

2

A Gold Pan, a Pick, and a Shovel

I wanted the gold and I sought it!
I scrabbled and mucked like a slave.
Was it famine or scurvy—I fought it;
I hurled my youth into a grave.
I wanted the gold and I got it—
Came out with a fortune last fall—
Yet somehow life's not what I thought it,
And somehow the gold isn't all.

THE SPELL OF THE YUKON—*Service*

F ree gold!" "Poor man's gold!" The Yukon had plenty of it. The only tools required to mine it were a gold pan, a pick, and a shovel.

Equally as necessary, however, were a strong back, patience, endurance, and optimism. The men who came to the North in the 1850s and '60s found that "Yukon digging" was the most primitive and

12

difficult type of mining in the world.

These early prospectors looked for what is known as "placer" gold. Placer deposits were formed when a vein of gold was eroded away by the force of a swiftly running stream. The freed ore fragments were carried along, then left in the bottom or along the side of the stream.

As streams changed their courses over the years, particles of gold were left in the old river beds. They were eventually scattered by wind and rain, or buried under silt, sand, and gravel. Thus, while gold could be found lying loose on the ground or in a stream, the bulk of the dust and nuggets were buried deep in the ground. It had sifted and worked its way down through the gravel and soil to the solid layer of rock—the bedrock—which lay several feet beneath the surface. There it lay, undisturbed for hundreds, or thousands, of years.

"PANNING" was the first in a long series of steps which led to this hidden treasure. To pan, the prospector used a container shaped like a pie pan to scoop some dirt and gravel from the bottom of a stream. He then moved the pan around and around until the dirt and water had sloshed over the sides. Gold is very heavy, and it remained on the bottom of the pan.

If there was eight or ten cents worth of gold

in his pan, that was "good prospects." The next step would be to sink a shaft.

The ground in the Yukon is frozen solid the year round. Even in the middle of summer only the top foot or two is thawed by the sun. Then the land becomes a slimy, boggy marsh. If a man tried to dig a hole in it, the hole would fill up with mud and water faster than he could dig. For that reason, shafts were usually dug in the winter.

First, the miner built a fire about four feet across. He let it burn until the top layer of ground was thawed. After scraping it away, he built another fire and repeated the burning and the scraping. A shaft was usually two-and-a-half feet wide and six feet long. It had to reach all the way down to bedrock, which might be twenty feet below the surface of the ground. If a man shoveled, picked, and burned ten inches a day toward bedrock, he considered it a good day's work.

As he worked his way downward, there came a time when he could no longer throw the dirt out of the hole. Then he had to stop and build a windlass so he could hoist it out. At this point it was good to have a partner. Otherwise, he had to climb out of the hole to empty the bucket, then down again to fill it.

He still wasn't finished when he finally reached bedrock. Now it was time for the "drifting." Drifting was digging tunnels into the sides of the shaft. The fire was relit and the dirt chipped and picked away until the miner had enough of a sample to tell whether he had hit a "skunk" or "paydirt."

If it was a skunk, it meant that he had to sink another shaft in another location. Then there were more endless days spent in the dark, stifling, smoke-filled hole; more buckets of dirt to be hauled with aching muscles into the freezing weather awaiting him on the surface; more choking, gasping, wheez-ing, sweating, and freezing to be endured.

If he was fortunate enough to see good "color" in the drifts, he went to work with renewed energy. The dirt and gravel which he hauled out were placed in a "dump," or a pile. The dump immedi-ately froze and remained that way until spring.

When the dump thawed out, it was time for the "clean-up." Lumber had to be hauled from the nearest sawmill, or trees must be cut down and planks made. Then the "sluice boxes" or "rockers" had to be built. A sluice box was a long, narrow trough which was placed on trestles in a swiftly running stream. The water was allowed to rush through and out of the trough as the dirt was shov-eled into it. The gold settled to the bottom and was caught on "riffles" or crossbars which were nailed on the inside of the box.

If the stream was sluggish or there wasn't

enough water, a rocker was used. This was a box about four feet long which was attached to wooden rockers. On top there was a metal plate punched full of small holes. Below the metal plate were some riffles which were covered with pieces of blanket.

As the dirt and water were poured on the metal plate, the box was rocked to and fro. The gold sifted through the holes and was caught on the blanket as the muddy water sloshed out over the sides of the box. As slow and awkward as rocking was, two partners using this method could clean up over a hundred dollars worth of gold a day.

MANY MONTHS passed between the time the first panning was done and the final ounce of gold was washed out of the last bucket of gravel. They were dreary, exhausting months. There may have been days or weeks when there hadn't been anything to eat except beans and biscuits. There might have been days when the temperature was too low to work the mine. At such times it seemed as if the walls of the cabin were closing in and suffocating the men who were confined there. Tempers grew short and exploded for the smallest reason. Harmless habits—the cracking of knuckles, the grinding of teeth, the drumming of fingers on a table—jabbed at raw nerves. There were men who shouted angry, bitter words, and drew a line down the center of the cabin. For the rest of the winter each man lived on his side of the line without speaking another word.

When the weather warmed up, one of them packed up and moved on by himself. Often, neither made any attempt to patch up the friendship. It had been a victim of the winter.

There were two men who got through the winter by keeping a moose in their cabin. Such a roommate undoubtedly caused some problems, but he gave the men something to think about beside the howling wind and the constant darkness that surrounded them.

Great pains were taken to make certain the fire in the Yukon stove was kept burning. As the warmth built up, the green logs of the cabin walls started to steam. If the fire went out, the steam would freeze and spread out in a sheet of ice on the dirt floor.

On the other hand, the biting cold could be used to weatherproof the cabin. Windows were securely plugged by filling them with chunks of ice. The chinks between the logs were stuffed with moss, then sprayed with water. The ice that formed made an airtight seal until the weather turned warm.

Scurvy and tuberculosis and frostbite were common, and men took them in their stride. Many of them made their fortunes after years of work, only to die within a short time, their bodies ravaged and worn out. In the spring, lifeless men were found along streams or in remote cabins.

BLIZZARDS, heartache, death—the Yukon had all of these. It also had exhilarating beauty, opportunities for adventure, and freedom from crowding and pressure. It was possible for January to have days when it was warm enough to shed bulky outer garments. When the hunting was good, there were banquets of moosemeat and grouse, ending with berry pies. Men visited each other's cabins and formed lifelong friendships. They went into town to play cards or to discuss Shakespeare and Kipling at a meeting of the literary society.

Some men took Indian wives and built neat, permanent cabins with vegetable gardens in the backyard. Many of them sent their children to private schools in the United States. Men who had wives back home sent for them. Schools and churches were built.

Single men organized dances and parties and invited Indian girls. The laughter and music lasted on and on into the endless winter nights.

Then there was the spree, which was the high point of the year. It was the time when the cleanup was over and a man wanted to see how fast he could empty his poke. Everyone who wanted to join in followed him to the nearest saloon. The bartenders were threatened by clubs in the hands of the fun-seekers. The man in charge of the spree helped himself to the liquor and cigars, treating everyone in the crowd.

At the height of the spree the miners might line up on two sides of the saloon and throw firewood at each other. Then someone would jump up on the bar to make a speech. Someone else would upset the water barrel. Then perhaps the stove would be turned over. It steamed and crackled as it made contact with the water on the floor.

When the spree was over, the man who had started it handed his poke of gold to the saloonkeeper and asked him to take out the amount of the damages. A good spree could last several days. One bill for damages came to almost three thousand dollars. No one ever regretted the time or money spent in this manner. After the months of unrelenting work and isolation, a man considered the spree to be a necessary ritual. Now, exhausted, happy, and probably broke, he was willing to find another sandbar and start his search again.

A MAN could find whatever he wanted in the Yukon Valley. He could find desolation and endless stretches of snow and ice. He could find spruce forests and clear rivers. He could find loneliness, or he could find companionship. He could find solitude and peace of mind or bleak despair.

It all depended on what he brought with him and what he expected to find there. A sourdough's life was what he made it.

THIS STATE of affairs was not destined to continue. Among those working in the valley in the early 1880s there were four notable men. Arthur Harper was one of them. The others were Leroy Napoleon McQueston, Joseph Ladue, and Arthur Mayo. They were setting in motion a series of events which in just a few years was to turn the eyes of the world upon the Northland.

3

The Men Behind the Miners

At Circle, Bill, when we wuz broke,
    Way back in Ninety-Four
When all our flour and beans wuz gone,
    An' we went back for more—
What wuz it ol' McQueston sed,
    As we put it up to him?
How we wanted a nuther chance
    Though the chance wuz mighty slim?
"Why, he'p perselves, my boys," sez he.
    "Go out an' hit the pay:
An' when you've got it sure enough,
    Just stroll aroun' my way."

—*A. Sauerdo*

A large group of men stood on the dock, anxiously awaiting the arrival of Jack McQueston's steamer. It was the only lifeline they had to the Outside. When it was spotted coming down the river, there were cheers and gunshots to welcome it. The men's mouths watered as they thought of the fresh fruits, eggs, and milk which it carried.

The unloading process seemed endless. The men started milling around and grumbling. McQueston, a big, ruddy-faced blond man, knew how they felt. He decided to speed things up.

"Come on over here," he called heartily. "Just help yourselves and keep a list of what you take. You can pay me when you get around to it."

Within an hour the men had gathered up what they needed and disappeared. McQueston made no effort to keep track of what was taken, but when the final tally was made, the only item missing was a carton containing six cans of condensed milk.

A STRANGE way of doing business? Perhaps, but that was how Jack McQueston earned his title, "Father of the Yukon."

He and Arthur Harper and Al Mayo had gone into partnership when they decided that it was possible they would never find their bonanza. None of them ever gave up prospecting entirely, but their string of trading posts kept them from going broke. Their log cabin stores were popular gathering places. Men came to buy flour, beans, blankets, rifles, and liniment. They stayed to sit around the big black wood stove and swap tales of narrow escapes from hungry bears and wolves and swirling rapids. They talked about gold—the latest strike and rumors about the next strike, how good the panning was in nearby creeks, and their disappointment at running into a "skunk" after weeks of sinking a shaft. They poured out their frustrations and swore they were going to leave the territory when the river ice broke. Then after finding a sympathetic ear and receiving a word of encouragement, they decided to go on and try one more sandbar.

HARPER eventually took on another partner, Joe Ladue, a stocky, swarthy Frenchman. Ladue's shrewd mind saw the possibilities in the desolate land and the men who wandered it. He became a one-man Chamber of Commerce for the entire Yukon Valley.

"I hear they're ankle-deep in nuggets a few miles downriver," he'd say. His words always touched off a spark of gold fever in the men who heard him. Almost before they realized it, Ladue would have them outfitted and on their way to the new strike.

He had a special reason for wanting to make a fortune. His sweetheart was waiting for him back in New York. He cringed whenever he remembered her father's angry parting words.

"You're nothing but a penniless drifter," he'd shouted. "I will not give my permission for you to marry my daughter!"

Ladue was determined to prove that he was worthy of her. He was going to become wealthy and return home to claim his bride.

McQUESTON, Mayo, Harper, and Ladue—these four men, more than any others, opened up the Yukon. Since the prospectors now had reliable sources of food and supply, they could throw all of their energies into locating new gold fields. The trading post operators directed men to the latest strike, then followed them, opening up a new trading post, and establishing a town.

McQueston's first post was at Fort Reliance. Perhaps it was an omen that it was located just six miles from the mouth of the Klondike River. This trading post became the focus for many future river settlements. As men poled their way through the white, foaming water, barely making it past jutting points of rock, and fighting to stay afloat as whirlpools clutched at their frail rafts, their muscles ached more with each mile of progress they made. As they passed each tributary on the way to Fort Reliance, they said to themselves, "Only seventy more miles to go . . . only forty more miles to go . . . only twelve more miles to go."

The tributaries became known as Seventymile, Sixtymile, Fortymile, and Twelvemile, and the towns that grew at their mouths also took those names.

McQUESTON bought a steamer that was able to make two trips inland every summer before the river froze. If there wasn't enough food brought in on those two trips, there was the possibility of starvation in the valley before a year went by.

In the spring of 1886, McQueston went to San Francisco to order supplies to stock his trading posts. While he was gone gold was discovered at Fortymile. Harper had just opened a new store nearby at the mouth of the Stewart River. When he saw the men rushing off to the new strike, he realized that word would leak out and there would be a torrent of men coming over the Chilkoot Pass in the spring. He had to get word to McQueston to order more supplies. The only way to do that would be to notify the storekeeper at the coastal town of Dyea. He, in turn, could put a message on a ship bound for San Francisco.

But it was January. Who could he find who would be fool enough to attempt the suicidal five-hundred-mile journey in the middle of winter?

"Might as well be in a soundproof prison," he said in despair. Winter had sealed off the whole valley from the outside world.

Finally, a steamboat captain named George Williams and an Indian boy volunteered. They set off with a team of dogs and a sled piled high with food and blankets. There would be no place to restock their provisions until they arrived at Dyea.

As they ran along after the dogs, their feet and legs quickly grew sore as they broke through the thin crust of snow and made contact with the jagged, rocky surface of the ground. Sharp pieces of ice like pieces of broken glass tore at their boots until they hung in shreds. They bound their feet in rags, which became bloodsoaked as their raw skin rubbed and chafed. Their lungs ached as they breathed the frigid air.

Ice collected between the dogs' toes and they slowed and faltered as it cut into their feet. The men had to halt and remove the ice by taking the paws into their own mouths and melting the ice with their breath.

The food supply dwindled and by March the dogs had all either starved to death or been frozen by the icy winds that swept over the plains. Stumbling, crawling, and creeping, the men kept on until they had reached the summit of the Chilkoot Pass. There a screeching blizzard and the blackness of the night made it impossible to go on. With numb, bleeding hands they clawed out a cave in a

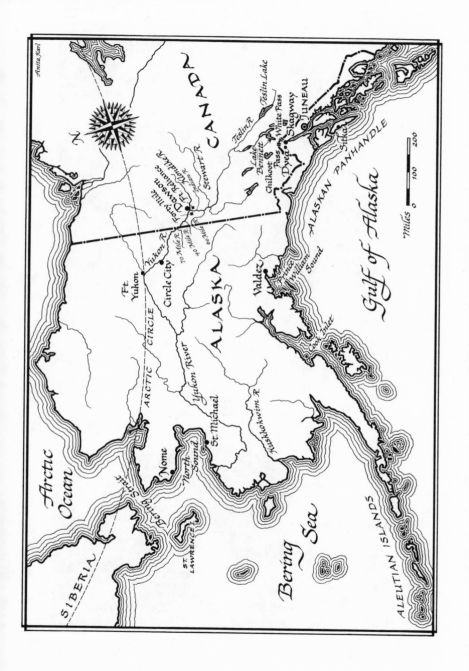

A prospector hitting the trail.

A tired cheechako.

The clean-up. Miners in the Yukon Valley washing out their gold.

A miner's cabin in the Klondike Valley

A typical dog team.

A dog carrying supplies to the goldfields.

A pan of gold dust.

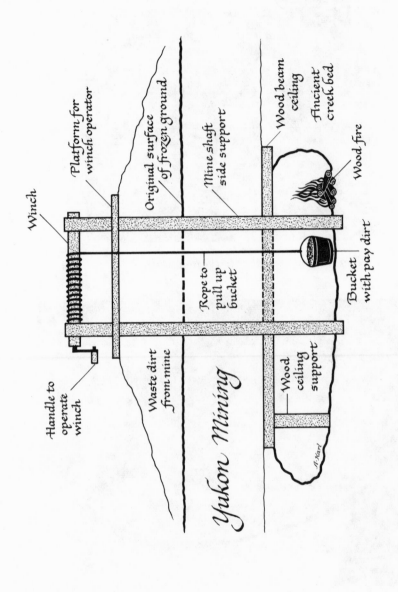

Yukon Mining

Winch

Handle to operate winch

Platform for winch operator

Original surface of frozen ground

Waste dirt from mine

Mine shaft side support

Rope to pull up bucket

Wood ceiling support

Wood beam ceiling

Ancient creek bed

Wood fire

Bucket with pay dirt

Operating a gold rocker, Skookum Hill, Dawson 1898.

Sluicing to wash out the gold from the dirt.

Panning gravel for gold indoors at 50° below zero—Dawson

A Yukon River steamer.

snowbank and huddled inside of it for three days. They had only a few handfuls of flour to eat and by the end of the third day, even that was gone. By then, Williams' legs were useless because of frostbite.

When the storm died down, the Indian carried Williams down the trail to the timberline. There, overcome by fatigue, he was forced to lay him in the snow and to stumble on alone hoping to find help. He startled a group of men when he appeared like an apparition out of the swirling wind-driven snow.

The men brought Williams into Dyea, where he died without speaking a word. The Indian managed to gasp out his message in broken English, and word was sped to McQueston. It arrived in time to avert the threatened starvation.

WHEN McQueston returned the following summer, he established the town of Fortymile. It was typical of most such towns. Miners gathered there in the winter when they had no claims to work. They built cabins in haphazard rows and passed the time discussing domestic and foreign affairs as well as playing cards and talking about gold. They read everything they could lay their hands on—a year-old newspaper or books on science and philosophy.

Wives and children moved in as the town grew. Small businesses were started—dressmaking shops, watchmakers, and blacksmiths along with the saloons and gambling halls. Schools and churches appeared, and the streets were busy with pedestrians and horsedrawn carts.

However, on the coldest winter days, life slowed down, then came to a standstill. People kept two vials outside their cabin doors. One contained mercury. When it froze only the hardiest ventured outside. The other contained Davis Painkiller, which was almost pure alcohol. When that froze it meant that it was at least seventy-two degrees below zero. Then only the sled dogs roamed the deserted streets.

These dogs were ravenous creatures and would eat anything in sight. They gobbled down leather gloves and boots, harnesses, snowshoes, pots of paste, and brushes. One dog ate a whole dishrag for the grease in it. Another ate a candle, flame and all. They ate cakes of soap and tore open cans of salmon with their bare teeth.

Men placed a high value on their dogs. They were their transportation and their companions when there were no other humans around. They were warmth on a winter trail as men lay curled around them on beds of spruce branches.

Towns such as Fortymile had no mayors, no judges, nor police. The miner's meetings provided whatever decisions were necessary. As the town grew, however, the Northwest Mounted Police appeared. Their law, while many times shaped to fit the situation, was usually strict and unbending. Many sourdoughs, feeling fenced in, started packing. In Fortymile, the discovery of gold at Preacher's Creek near the Arctic Circle provided the reason to move on. McQueston followed soon after and founded Circle City, which came to be known as the Paris of the North, the largest log cabin town in the world.

WHILE Circle City flourished, there were at least two men in the valley who did not care to follow the crowds. Robert Henderson was one of them. He preferred to prospect along streams which other men had not yet worked. Another was George Carmack. He had married an Indian girl and turned "siwash"—content to live like a native. Fishing and hunting filled his hours.

It was while Carmack was fishing in a salmon stream with an unpronounceable Indian name that Robert Henderson happened to see him. Their meeting was to lead to the greatest stampede the Northland had ever seen.

4

Two Men, Each With a Dream

In the early days we were just a few,
  And we hunted and fished around,
Nor dreamt by our lonely campfires of the
  Wealth that lay under the ground.
We traded in skins and whisky,
  And I've often slept under the shade
Of that lone birch tree on Bonanza
  Where the first big find was made.

We were just like a great big family,
  And every man had his squaw,
And we lived such a wild, free, fearless life,
  Beyond the pale of the law;
Till sudden there came a whisper,
  And it maddened us, every man,
And I got in on Bonanza
  Before the big rush began.

THE PARSON'S SON—*Service*

That's just ol' Lyin' George again, telling his whoppers. What can you expect from a siwash?"

George Carmack was used to the snickers and taunts. Hunting for gold didn't interest him. However, when he happened to find a few nuggets in a stream, he liked to brag about it. As for being called siwash, he was proud of the name. He was even beginning to look like a native, with his droopy, black mustache and his round, jowly face. His hair and skin were oily and had a fishy smell because he ate so much salmon.

He believed in omens and spirits. One night in July, 1896, he dreamed he was standing by a stream. The salmon were leaping high over the water on their way to the spawning grounds. Suddenly, two huge fish jumped high in the air and landed on the ground at his feet. They had golden nuggets instead of scales and golden coins for eyes.

Carmack thought that this dream meant that he was due to have good luck fishing. If he caught a lot of salmon, he could dry it and sell it for dog food. The next day he and two of his Indian friends, Skookum Jim and Tagish Charlie, went fishing on the Klondike River.

ROBERT HENDERSON also had a dream. He was a tall, lean Scotsman with piercing eyes and a full mustache. His dream was of finding a fortune in gold, and he had spent most of his life prospecting his way around the world. He was proud of his way of life and wore his wide-brimmed miner's hat everywhere he went.

However, he was discouraged when he walked into Ladue's trading post at Sixtymile one day in 1894. He sat at the rickety table and stared dully at the grimy walls which were covered with pictures from old newspapers. Maybe these store owners have the right idea, he thought. It's foolish to waste my life chasing gold.

Ladue served him some tea and beans. He sensed Henderson's despondency. "I hear there's good prospects on the Indian River," he said cheerfully. "Nuggets as big as your thumbnail. I'm so sure about it that I'll grubstake you if you want to try it."

Ladue's optimism filled Henderson with hope. "If it's good for me, then it'll be good for you," he said as the two shook hands. "I'm a determined man."

Henderson moved from creek to sandbar in the Indian River Valley. He found gold many times, but it was never enough to satisfy him. In the summer he suffered the torture of leg cramps from standing in chilling streams. In the winter he endured bouts of snow blindness. He once fell across the broken branch of a tree and it impaled his leg. For fourteen days he lay in his tent fighting infection and fever. Then he limped off to do some more panning, his injured leg filled with dull spurts of pain.

When he had his strength back, he decided to climb a domelike mountain. He had long been curious about what lay on the other side of it. When he reached the summit, he stood entranced for several minutes. Spread out before him was the most beautiful view he had ever seen. From the base of the mountain six streams fanned out in all directions. Upon their banks moose grazed peacefully on lush green grasses.

Henderson didn't know it, but he was looking down upon the Klondike Valley. To the west beyond the rolling hills was Rabbit Creek. He might have entered the valley if he hadn't seen the moose. Moose pastures always had mosquitoes and thick, black, oozy mud. And besides, it was a well-known fact that there was no gold to be found where moose grazed.

He scrambled down to a small creek in a gorge a few yards down the side of the mountain. Scooping up some mud with his gold pan, he sloshed it around until he could detect the gold in the bottom. There was eight cents worth there. He felt the familiar flush of excitement at the sight of good prospects. Maybe he had found what he had been looking for!

True to the Yukon Code he retraced his steps and told several men about his discovery. Three of them returned with him. By July of 1896, they had taken out seven hundred and fifty dollars' worth of gold. Henderson named the creek Gold Bottom, then headed back to Sixtymile to lay in the winter's supplies. He told everyone he saw about the strike. By the time Ladue had finished filling his order, Henderson and the storekeeper were the only ones left in town.

Henderson decided against taking the Indian River back to Gold Bottom. The water was low and the bottom of his skin boat would have been torn to shreds by rocks. Instead, he continued down the Yukon to the Klondike. As he poled his way back to his claim he spotted Carmack and the two Indians fishing on the bank. He stopped and told Carmack about his strike.

"What are the chances to locate up there?" asked Carmack. "Is everything staked?"

Henderson glanced at the Indians and lowered his voice. "There's a chance for you, but I don't want any siwashes staking on that creek."

"Well, I might give it a try in a few days," replied Carmack.

As Carmack watched Henderson continue on down the river, he felt a burning resentment grow within him. The Scotsman had insulted his friends. That was something which would be hard to forget. He said to the Indians that he didn't think he wanted to go to Gold Bottom at all. Skookum Jim, however, was a much more ambitious man than Carmack. If there was gold to be had, he wanted his share. He talked Carmack into looking at the new strike.

A few days later the three men started the journey. They struggled over thorny bushes and fallen trees and through thick underbrush. They floundered through a swamp where they sank to their knees in muck. Hundreds of gnats and mosquitoes swarmed about them, nipping at every inch of exposed skin.

Whenever they stopped to rest, they panned for gold in the various streams and creeks. At Rabbit Creek they saw what they considered good prospects. Carmack thought that it also looked like a good place to cut logs. He planned to float them downriver and sell them.

When they finally reached Gold Bottom, Carmack panned the stream half-heartedly, then decided to move on. Henderson had made it plain that he didn't want the Indians there. The last straw came when he refused to sell Charlie some tobacco, although he had plenty to spare.

As he left, however, Carmack, as was usual, promised Henderson that he would let him know about any good prospects he found.

Several days later Carmack and his friends were back on Rabbit Creek. They had shot a moose and were roasting hunks of the meat over a fire. Jim leaned over the creek to get a drink. He almost choked on the water when he saw what lay below the surface of the stream. There was more raw gold there than he had ever seen in one place. In a voice shrill with excitement, he called to Carmack and Charlie.

The three men peered into the water and saw pieces of gold wedged between the slabs of rock. They scooped some out. The first panful yielded an unbelievable amount—four dollars' worth.

"We did a war dance around that gold pan," said Carmack. "It was a combination Scotch horn-pipe, Indian fox trot, syncopated Irish jig, and a sort of siwash hula-hula."

The three friends could not sleep that night. They knew they had found what every prospector in the valley had dreamed of.

THE NEXT DAY was August 17. Carmack renamed the creek Bonanza and he and Charlie went to Fortymile to file their claims with the officials there.

Fortymile at that time was a town filled with poor men, every one of them down on their luck.

As much as they wanted gold, however, they were not ready to believe Lying George. When he announced his find to the sourdoughs in the saloon there were scornful mutters. "Gold at Rabbit Creek —that's a laugh. It's nothing but moose pasture . . . the beds are too wide . . . the hills are too low . . . the water doesn't taste right . . . the willows are leaning the wrong way."

Everyone in the saloon agreed that Rabbit Creek wasn't worth even a day of their time.

Carmack was exasperated. He pulled a sample of the gold he had panned. "Look," he said. "This is from just one panning."

The men laughed. "We know that Ladue gave you that gold. He'll do anything to start a stampede."

The laughter stopped as the gold was passed from hand to hand. It wasn't like any gold they had ever seen. It *must* have come from a new strike. One by one, the men made excuses to leave the saloon. By midnight the stampede was in full force. By morning Fortymile was deserted.

When the first word reached Circle City, no one there believed it either. Then a few days later a letter arrived from someone the men trusted. Circle City was a dead town the following day.

From all over the Yukon territory sourdoughs and cheechakos were making their way to the Klondike Valley. At first the news had spread slowly with one man passing the word along to a friend. As each of these men stopped to buy supplies or to have a drink in a saloon, the word was spread still further. Prospectors who had been panning along lonely creeks packed their gear and headed for the Klondike. They told others along the way.

The news was shouted to men who were poling their boats up the Yukon River. Those men turned around and followed the growing crowd. Others did not hear about Bonanza, but they happened to pass by the mouth of the Klondike on their way to other creeks. When they saw all of the boats and men, they decided to stop and see what was happening.

By the end of August, Bonanza was staked out for fourteen miles. It seemed as if the only men who hadn't heard about the strike were Robert Henderson and the miners working with him at Gold Bottom.

5

The Wheel of Fortune

Now wouldn't you expect to find a man
an awful crank
That's staked out nigh three hundred
claims and every one a blank;
That's followed every fool stampede, and
seen the rise and fall
Of camps where men got gold in chunks
and he got none at all;
That's prospected a bit of ground and sold
it for a song;
To see it yield a fortune to some fool that
came along;
That's sunk a dozen bed-rock holes, and
not a speck in sight,
Yet sees them take a million out from the
claims to left and right?

THE BALLAD OF HARD-LUCK HENRY—*Service*

WW ithin a week of Carmack's discovery, the
Klondike Valley was a scene of mass confusion.
Men rammed their stakes in anywhere, jumped each

39

other's claims, and argued and scrambled for ground. Boats piled up at the mouth of the river. Tents sprang up where just a few days earlier moose had grazed.

Almost the only ones who actually believed that there was gold at bedrock as well as on the surface were the cheechakos. Many of the sourdoughs staked only from force of habit. Having done that, they failed to record their claim or sold it for little or nothing. If they had enough food they stayed on for a while. They had all been fooled too many times by good surface prospects, but some of the old timers believed that it was their last chance to be part of a stampede. They wandered aimlessly up and down the valley, hypnotized by the activity and excitement. One of them found an unclaimed plot and put up a sign.

THIS MOOSE PASTURE RESERVED
FOR SWEDES AND CHEECHAKOS.

He chuckled, certain that he knew worthless land when he saw it.

Many sourdoughs did not enter the valley. One of them looked at the men slogging around in the swamp and turned away in disgust. "I wouldn't go across the river on that old siwash's word," he said to his companion. "This whole thing is just a stunt put on by Ladue and Harper to drum themselves up some business."

BY THE END of August all of Bonanza was staked and men were fanning out across the watershed looking for more ground. Antone Stander, a handsome, dark-haired Austrian, was one of these. He had sought his fortune all over North America, then walked thousands of miles into the Yukon. He had no money and little food. If he didn't strike gold, he had no idea how he would get through the winter.

When he stumbled upon a little trickle of water at the south fork of Bonanza, he halfheartedly scooped up a panful of gravel. He sloshed the mud out, stared at what was left, blinked, then stared again. Six dollars worth of gold! Why, this was better than Bonanza! This was Eldorado—a place of great riches!

Stander was so caught up with his discovery that he barely noticed a group of men approaching.

"Any good prospects?" one of them asked.

Stander shoved the pan of gold out of sight. "Nothing—nothing worth mentioning," he replied in a shaky voice. He couldn't bring himself to share his good fortune.

The stampede was just starting and already the Yukon Code was being discarded.

As soon as the men had left, Stander dumped the contents of his pan into his poke. There was just enough gold to pay for his claim filing fee. But how was he going to get enough food and supplies so he could sink a shaft?

He went to the warehouse of the Alaska Commercial Company in Dawson and asked the officials there for credit. They refused his request, but told him if he could get someone to sign the loan with him they would give him what he needed.

Stander walked the streets despondently. He didn't know anyone well enough to ask such a favor. He entered the nearest saloon for a drink and started talking about his problem. Clarence Berry was the bartender on duty that night. He offered to sign the loan papers for the destitute Austrian.

Stander insisted on making Berry his partner. In less than a year both men were millionaires.

IN THE WINTER of 1896–7 enormous fortunes changed hands as easily as a can of beans. Poor men became rich and then poor again without even knowing it. One of the men who staked on Eldorado later sold his claim for a trifle. The man who bought it lived for fifty years on the gold he took from it.

Louis Rhodes mined the claim which was "Reserved for Swedes and Cheechakos." He went home the next spring with enough gold to support him in luxury for the rest of his life.

Charley Anderson was fast talked into buying a claim which was considered worthless. He paid eight hundred dollars for it—all the money he had in the world. When he realized what he had done, he tried to get out of the deal, but everyone laughed at him and called him a "dumb Swede."

When Anderson cleaned up his dump in the spring, he was worth a million dollars.

Thomas Lippy staked a claim above the timber line. He then traded it for one near a clump of trees because his wife wanted him to build a cabin. His first claim contained no gold. His second produced a million and a half dollars.

Alex McDonald gave a starving man a sack of flour for his "worthless" claim. After several more such deals, McDonald was worth $20 million and was called "King of the Yukon."

WHILE the wheel of fortune was spinning in the Klondike Valley, Robert Henderson was working a claim which had showed him the best prospects he had even seen—thirty-five cents a pan. He and his partners had not seen any other white man since Carmack had walked away saying that he would send word back if he saw anything interesting on Rabbit Creek.

One day Henderson saw some men coming

over the hill. He waved to them. "Where did you come from?" he called.

"Bonanza Creek," one of them replied. "It's right back there." He pointed back over the hill.

"That's Rabbit Creek," said Henderson, feeling the first faint stirrings of alarm. "What's happening over there?"

"The biggest thing in the world," was the answer. "But it's all staked out. Carmack found it a month ago."

Henderson was stunned. Then as the shock left him, rage and frustration such as he had never felt filled his entire body. He threw his shovel down and stared at the ground. For over an hour his mind was in turmoil. Why, Carmack wasn't even a prospector —just a lazy, fishy-smelling siwash. He had struck it rich and then had broken his promise. It wasn't right! It wasn't fair! He, himself, had been looking all of his life, and thirty-five cents a pan was the best he'd ever found.

Henderson spent the rest of his years looking for his bonanza, but he never found it. He died a bitter and brokenhearted man.

LADUE closed his post in Sixtymile and followed the strike. When he reached the mouth of the Klondike and saw the tents and boats piled up there, he knew that the chance he'd awaited for fourteen years was at hand. He paced out a townsite and erected a sawmill, a trading post, and a saloon. The town of Dawson sprang to life as quickly as if someone had waved a magic wand. Houses were built, the Mounties established a headquarters, and dance halls, barber shops, and restaurants were crowded with men and women seeking entertainment and services. The muddy streets were churned to an oozy slime beneath the boots of hundreds of people.

As the winter of 1896–7 approached, the activity slowed. The men who had not staked a claim huddled in their cabins or tried to relieve the monotony by getting drunk. Those who were sinking shafts lived lives of unremitting labor and hardship. Never had rich men lived so poorly. They slept in lean-tos, huts, and crude cabins. Their mattresses were spruce twigs laid out on frozen ground. To relight their fires, they had to crawl from their sleeping bags into fifty-below-zero weather. They did not bathe from fall until spring, and lice thrived in their hair and blankets. They ate beans and hardtack and their teeth loosened from scurvy.

Many of them had no experience with a northern winter. Some of them carelessly wandered too far from their shelters and found themselves growing sleepy. Soon the snow looked like a warm, downy mattress. Many men rested for "just a moment" and their frozen bodies were found along the trail from Dawson to Bonanza.

One man was lucky enough to be rescued from such a death. He later wrote about his experience.

My eyelids kept freezing together, but I had to be careful about pulling off my gloves to thaw them apart. I did it as quickly as I could, but several times my hands nearly froze before I could get them back in the big mitten.

By spring there were fifteen hundred people in the Klondike Valley. One thousand more had crossed the Chilkoot and were waiting at Lake Bennett for the ice on the Yukon River to break. At noon on May 14, 1897 there was the long awaited ear-shattering crack. Then to the accompaniment of men's shouts of glee, cakes of ice as big as houses rumbled, roared, and crashed as they started moving slowly out to sea. Two days later the river was navigable and an armada of small boats was on its way to Dawson. Within two weeks the town had doubled in size.

As THE NEWCOMERS arrived, the men who had been cleaning up were beginning to celebrate. They were rich beyond their wildest dreams. Uppermost in their minds was the desire to return home where they could enjoy their wealth.

Early in June two sternwheelers arrived bringing food for the hungry population. When they left they carried eighty dirty, tired, homesick passengers. One of them was Joe Ladue, who was going to New York to claim his bride. Some of them had not seen civilization for years. None of them had had any contact with the outside world since the previous summer. These passengers carried with them three tons of gold. They had it packed in suitcases, cartons, sacks, jam jars, baking powder tins, and in ragged blankets tied with frayed rope.

At St. Michael on the Bering Sea they transferred to two southbound steamers—the *Portland*, which was headed for Seattle and the *Excelsior*, bound for San Francisco. The docking of these ships in the States was to set up an electrifying chain of events which would soon extend around the world.

6

"A Ton of Gold!"

GOLD! WE LEAPED *from our benches.* GOLD!
We sprang from our stools.
GOLD! *We whirled in the furrow, fired with
the faith of fools.*
*Fearless, unfound, unfitted, far from the night
and the cold,*
*Heard we the clarion summons, followed the
master lure—*GOLD!

THE TRAIL OF NINETY-EIGHT—*Service*

Late in the afternoon of July 14, 1897, a grimy
ship slipped quietly into San Francisco Bay. The
men who disembarked looked even grimier than the
ship. Their lined faces were burned almost black,
and their whiskers were scraggly and dirty. Their
tattered boots were held together with rope, and
their trousers and jackets caked with mud.

There were a few women among them. They
were dressed in ill-fitting men's clothes and their

skin looked like brown shoeleather. Their hands were rough and cracked with ground-in dirt, and their fingernails broken.

Curious knots of bystanders gathered on the dock to watch the strange procession come down the gangplank. Every passenger grappled with tattered luggage and stumbled under the weight of bulging suitcases.

A faint whisper made its way through the people on the dock. Could the rumors about a gold strike somewhere up north be true? What were these people carrying in those bags?

The whisper became a murmur. More people came to watch as a group of the passengers hired a four-horse truck and heaved their baggage into it.

"Take us to the nearest smelting works," one of them directed the driver.

Smelting works! It was true! The word gold was passed from lip to lip and soon the dock was crowded with shouting men. They surged behind the truck, followed it to the smelting works, then stood goggle-eyed while the buckskin bags, the soiled canvas sacks, and the glass jars were emptied onto the counter.

The crowd grew silent with awe as the gold lay there in front of them, "like a pile of shelled corn."

*　*　*

WITHIN MINUTES the news had spread throughout San Francisco. By the next day newspapers all over the country had printed the story. When the *Portland*, the second gold ship, reached Seattle on July 16, the town was already aflame with gold fever. A tugboat full of reporters sailed out to meet the ship when it appeared on the horizon. Then the tug raced back to port and three extras hit the streets almost as soon as the *Portland* docked. The headlines shouted

GOLD! GOLD! GOLD! GOLD!
68 Rich Men on
the Steamer *Portland*
STACKS OF YELLOW METAL!

Within twenty-four hours a phrase from one of the articles, "a ton of gold," was being flashed around the world.

EACH MINER was interviewed over and over. As the tales they told were repeated, each listener heard only the facts he wanted to hear. "All you need is a pan and plenty of water." "He said he got his gold out in twenty-six days." "Two tenderfeet knocked over a boulder and found eight hundred dollars' worth of nuggets." "Without practically a stroke two partners came out with twenty-five thousand dollars apiece." "There are nuggets as big as potatoes."

No one seemed to hear about fifty-below-zero weather, or that the Klondike was already completely staked out, or that the journey over the Chilkoot was tortuous and dangerous.

No one asked what placer mining was like. They wanted to believe that three tons of gold had simply washed out of a creek and into the miners' pans. To the hungry, jobless population of the depression-ridden United States, it was a glorious solution to their problems.

A FEW HOURS after the arrival of the *Portland*, Seattle had gone "stark, raving mad," according to one reporter. The streets were so jammed with people that the streetcars couldn't run. That was just as well, because the conductors were quitting and booking passage north. Policemen resigned, salesmen leaped over their counters, preachers left their congregations. The mayor quit to form a steamship company. Tickets on northbound vessels were selling for one thousand dollars to fifteen hundred dollars instead of the usual two hundred dollars.

Joining in the stampede were thugs, gamblers, and confidence men. A man named Jefferson Randolph Smith was among them.

Ten days later fifteen hundred people had

already left Seattle for the gold fields, and there were nine more ships in the harbor loaded and ready to sail. The streets and docks were packed with frantic men, women, and children twenty-four hours a day. They slept in stables and washed at fire hydrants. Every hotel was full, restaurants were overtaxed, and supply houses remained open day and night.

The downtown streets were lined with piles of clothing, tools, and food. Goats, sheep, horses, oxen, and dogs were tethered in vacant lots. Dog owners had to lock their pets up or they would be stolen. The stampeders seemed to think that any stray mutt could be trained to be a sled dog.

In one great stroke the depression ended in Seattle and San Francisco. Business boomed as it had never boomed before. Woolen mills ran out of blankets and heavy clothing. Evaporated food plants couldn't keep up with the demand. Hardware stores couldn't order enough picks and shovels.

Within a month the boom was affecting the rest of the country. Anything was salable if it had the name "Klondike" attached to it. There were Klondike glasses, boots, medicine chests, stoves, blankets, and bicycles. The stampeders snapped up gasoline-powered sleds, steam-driven automatic gold pans, scurvy and frost cures, felt-lined portable cabins, containers of mosquito killing germs, X-ray machines that would detect the presence of gold, and machines to suck the gold from river beds.

No device or idea was too wild to sell. A man sold shares in a carrier pigeon scheme which promised quick communication with the gold fields. Balloons were sold which would enable men to float their supplies over the mountains. Women signed up to join a boatload of brides-to-be. The promoter assured them that they would find a rich husband as soon as they stepped off the boat. Other women, more practical or perhaps less romantic, rushed north to open restaurants and laundries.

Hundreds of people gave money to a man who was raising gophers and training them to claw holes through the gravel and down to bedrock.

The unfortunate people who couldn't join the stampeders grubstaked friends or complete strangers, or bought stock in mining and steamship companies.

Every available ship was rushed into service to accommodate the thousands of waiting passengers. When all of the freighters, ferry boats, yachts, barges, and fishing schooners were gone, rusty, unseaworthy vessels were pulled out of ships' graveyards all along the west coast. A small fleet of boats left the East coast to join the fleet. Crews were hired with only the briefest examination of their seaman's papers.

Many times two tickets were sold for every space available, so the passengers had to scramble aboard and fight for room. Sharp-pointed picks and shovels protruding from bags slung over men's backs poked and prodded the people around them. Some ships had so many passengers crammed on board that there was not enough room to carry a sufficient amount of fuel for the trip. Some had no compasses and many had no refrigeration. Faulty boilers threatened to blow up, and several eventually did.

One old coal tanker was pressed into service so quickly that it was still full of coal dust. During the passage the dust clung to the passengers and coated their lungs. Rough berths filled every cranny, and three or four people slept in a space meant for one. Eight hundred men, women, and children shared the small ship with three hundred horses. There was so much hay piled on the deck that it cut off the pilot's forward view.

There were eating facilities for only sixty-five people. Passengers lined up to eat the sickening food, and as soon as one person had gulped his meal down, another slid in to take his place. To reach the table they had to brush up against two sides of raw beef which had been hung on the wall.

The floor quickly became covered with refuse which was never swept up—only sprinkled with wood shavings to hide it. The passengers were quartered under rough plank decks upon which the horses were tethered and the excretions of the animals leaked through the cracks onto the bunks. There was no air circulation and the animal stench combined with the smell of seasickness to make the atmosphere unbearable. Most passengers crowded onto the upper decks so they could breathe. There they stood in driving rain and wind, since there was no seating or shelter for them.

A FEW warning voices tried to quiet the hysteria which had swept the country. United States government officials issued a plea to stop the travel. "Winter is coming," they said. "There are already thousands of people at the pass who can't get over. Skagway and Dyea are dangerously overcrowded."

The people of Skagway sent a petition to the Seattle Chamber of Commerce. "Stop the rush in the name of humanity."

Canadian officials sent out notice that their government could not accept responsibility for getting enough food into the Yukon.

Insurance companies cancelled the policies of anyone who joined the stampede.

The voices of caution were drowned out by the shouts of the railroads, steamship lines, and outfitting companies. They were becoming rich from the gold craze. They promised wealth, adventure, and romance to everyone who went to the Klondike.

Why should a man pay attention to any gloomy forebodings when he was being given a chance to make his wildest dreams come true?

7

Three Thousand Dead Horses

"Klondike or bust!" rang the slogan;
*   every man for his own*
Oh, how we flogged the horses, stagger-
*   ing skin and bone!*
Oh, how we cursed their weakness, an-
*   guish they could not tell,*
Breaking their hearts in our passion, lash-
*   ing them on till they fell!*

Oh, we were brutes and devils, goaded by
*   lust and fear!*
Our eyes were strained to the summit; the
*   weaklings dropped to the rear,*
Falling in heaps by the trail-side, heart-
*   broken, limp, and wan;*
But the gaps closed up in an instant, and
*   heedless the chain went on.*

THE TRAIL OF NINETY-EIGHT—*Service*

As the motley procession of ships was making its halting way up the coast, William Moore was tilling his farm three miles west of Dyea. He had staked out a townsite there in 1888, after first investigating the pass which led through the mountains at the edge of the property. The White Pass paralleled the Chilkoot and was ten miles longer, but it was six hundred feet lower and wide enough along its entire length for the use of pack animals.

Moore knew that it was a desirable alternate route to the gold fields. He built a cabin there, at Skagway, "the home of the wild wind," and waited patiently for the gold rush, which he was convinced would occur. The only thing he hadn't foreseen was the magnitude of the stampede.

On July 26, 1897, the first gold rush steamer arrived in Skagway Bay. It dumped its cargo of kicking horses, yelping dogs, and scrambling men, women, and children into the shallow waters. The invading horde heaped goods on the beach, tethered animals in the forest, erected tents and shacks, and cut down trees for firewood.

Vainly Moore shouted that the land was his, that he had a right to rental fees. Everyone ignored him. Within the next few hours several more ships arrived and he had no better luck with the people who poured out of them. Bewildered, Moore retired to his cabin to decide what to do next.

BY AUGUST tent saloons, restaurants, and outfitters were doing a thriving business. The beach was alive with swearing men, terrified horses, and hungry dogs. Hundreds of tents and mounds of supplies filled the beach. Small vessels scurried between ship and shore. They carried seasick passengers and their baggage, much of which had been smashed to pieces when it was thrown from the deck of the ship.

The bay was filled with thrashing goats, dogs, mules, and oxen that had been dumped overboard and left to fend for themselves.

On the slimy mudflats hundreds of men desperately hunted for the supplies which they had so carefully purchased two weeks earlier. Many times they found them after the tide had rushed in and soaked their furs, blankets, and sacks of flour and rice.

In an attempt to bring some order out of the chaos the business owners hired Frank Reid, an ex-Indian fighter, to survey the town and lay out roads. One of the planned roads went through Moore's cabin. He refused to move, but then backed down as a threatening crowd gathered. Still determined to make his land pay off, he built a pier which extended far out into the bay. Ships no longer had to dump passengers and cargo into the shallow water. By charging for its use Moore ended up with a steady income.

PEOPLE kept pouring into Skagway and the thousands who were already there frantically tried to replace lost and ruined food and equipment. The Mounties who guarded the Canadian border at the summit of the mountains had recommended that everyone bring a year's supply of food with them. Most people were trying to heed that advice. To earn the money for their provisions the stampeders ran errands, sawed lumber, unloaded boats, tended bar, and opened up blacksmith and watch repair shops.

A few hundred men decided to travel light and had gathered just enough food to last until they got over the pass. They were already making their way along the twenty-five mile trail. The first few miles wound gently over sloping pathways lined by shimmering pools and lush grasses. They strolled leisurely behind their heavily laden horsedrawn carts.

Then the trail grew steeper. Soon it was too narrow for the wagons, and goods had to be transferred to the backs of both men and animals. Within hours shoulder straps were biting into flesh, and leg and back muscles were aching. Breathing became labored and clothing which was damp from perspiration became clammy and ice cold as the wind whistled and the temperature dropped to thirty degrees lower than on the coast. Shivering bodies turned numb in the frigid air.

The trail started zigzagging as it went through canyons and over hills. It snaked between the steep gorges of the Skagway River and across slippery flanks of granite which sloped upward at a forty-five degree angle. Here horses scrambled for footing and men were forced to crawl on their hands and knees. Their hearts thudded achingly in their chests and their stomachs churned ominously.

The river crossed and recrossed the trail, and the climbers often had to ford its rushing waters. They then had to stop and dry out their clothes and to recover from frostbite, snow-blindness and nausea. They also nursed bruises and cuts and bound up sprained ankles. Then it was back to the trail, plunging ahead through slimy bogs and along narrow, precipitous pathways where one misstep could send a man to his death on the sharply pointed rocks five hundred feet below.

Blizzards struck without warning and the snow was like stinging pebbles. The wind screamed eerily and threw up a barrage of snow which cut off the view of the trail and darkened the skies.

Summit Hill was the last leg of the journey. It was a thousand foot climb that during the winter was slick with ice, and during the thaws was ankle deep in streaming rivulets of mud. Yawning mudholes that could swallow up a horse awaited the careless stampeder. There was no let-up from the hazards of the trail even as they crossed into Canada and the uniforms of the Northwest Mounted Police came into the line of vision.

By September of 1897 the dangers of mudslide and avalanche discouraged even the most foolhardy man from entering the White Pass. It became obvious that there was no chance to reach the Klondike until spring, because the Yukon River was frozen. Thousands of people were stranded in Skagway.

Hundreds of men came back down from the pass, having decided that no amount of gold was worth the struggle. It was common to see a man sitting beside his outfit, sobbing in despair. The tidal flats were covered with hundreds of horses with "For Sale" signs on their backs and blood streaming down their lacerated flanks. There was no market for the starving creatures even though boatloads of people were still arriving daily from the south.

Then the mud froze along the White Pass trail and the Skagway River turned to ice. A faint spark of hope once more flamed within the stampeders and they gathered their equipment together again. Word had come down the mountain that the Mounties' recommendation for a year's supply of food had become an order. This meant that each person had to transport about a ton of food and equipment to the gold fields. A man who depended entirely on his own back had to walk a total distance of twenty five hundred miles to get his gear over the twenty-five-mile pass. The trip involved ninety days of hauling sixty-five pounds of supplies up to a stopping point, caching it, then returning for another sixty-five pounds. In the meantime the snow was falling and burying his first load, so it had to be dug out when he was ready to repeat the operation to the next stopping point.

The gold hunters kept coming until there was a constant, unbroken stream of humanity extending all the way up the side of the mountain. No one dared stop. Every passing hour lessened the chance of staking a good claim. The strain caused tempers to flare and slight mishaps to turn into catastrophies. It was every man for himself. If the stampeder up ahead fell from illness or injury, no one heeded his cries. To the men who passed him by, his misfortune only meant that their chances were that much better.

If men suffered, the animals suffered even

more. They were overloaded, underfed, flogged, kicked, and knifed as their owners lost all human compassion. One man lit fires under a pair of oxen to make them move. Too exhausted to take another step, they burned alive. Another man angrily pushed his entire team of dogs into a hole in the river ice. They were swept off in the frigid water underneath. When their owner realized what he had done, he burst into hysterical sobs.

Three thousand horses perished on the White Pass trail that winter. Death came as a blessing. Their flanks and feet were torn by sharp rocks. They were disembowelled when they fell into mud-holes onto upended logs. They broke their legs when they stepped into small crevices. They suffered agonies when their skin was rubbed off down to the bone under their heavy packs. They were beaten and gouged by insane men who were trying to get them to move a few more feet before they fell for the last time. When it became obvious that they could no longer rise, the packs were stripped roughly from their backs, and they were left to die. Bullets were too precious to waste on a miserable animal.

One man was jabbing at his horse's flanks with a knife to make him keep moving. The creature hobbled to the edge of a precipice, looked down for a moment, and deliberately jumped. All who saw the incident knew that he had committed suicide.

MEANWHILE the few men who had reached Lake Bennett were out of food. They had money, however, so when they sighted a trading post they figured their troubles were over. To their surprise, the only items for sale were a few cans of condensed milk. They pushed off in their boats and floated off down the river, certain that the next trading post would supply their needs.

Suddenly they heard a disturbing cry from a man on the bank. "There's no grub in Dawson. If you haven't an outfit, for God's sake, turn back!"

8

Worthless Stacks of Gold

*Then a shuddery breath like the coming
    of Death crept down from the peaks
    far away;*
*The water was still; the twilight was
    chill; the sky was a tatter of gray.*
*Swift came the Big Cold, and opal and
    gold the lights of the witches arose;*
*The frost-tyrant clinched, and the valley
    was cinched by the stark and cadav-
    erous snows.*

THE BALLAD OF PIOUS PETE—*Service*

As soon as Joe Ladue had put up his first warehouse and sawmill, Dawson became the center of
social and business life in the Klondike Valley. In
January, 1897, there were only five houses there, but
dirty white tents were scattered between the trees.

By April there were fifteen hundred people living in the area. There were one thousand more stampeders constructing boats at Lake Bennett, which lay at the foot of the passes five hundred miles away. As soon as the river ice broke, they would be on their way to the gold fields.

From the first there was a shortage of everything except gold in Dawson. Salt fetched its weight in gold. A keg of blackened and bent nails rescued from a fire sold for eight hundred dollars. Many dogs had to be killed because there was not food enough to keep them alive.

During the winter there was little or no communication with the outside world. Certainly, none of the fifty thousand people headed toward the Klondike were aware of the seriousness of the situation there. William Ogilvie, a Canadian government surveyor stationed in Dawson, sensed that the population was going to increase tremendously in the next few months. He could foresee widespread starvation unless something was done quickly. With great difficulty he managed to send two messages to Ottawa, but no one there paid much attention to them.

In May of 1897, the ice broke on the Yukon. Within a short time two hundred boats had arrived at Dawson. Day and night more vessels streamed in until the town held thirty-five hundred people. Buildings were sprouting up everywhere and no one except Ogilvie and a few merchants seemed to worry about the fact that there wasn't much to buy with the gold everyone hoped to find.

In early June two steamers arrived. As the crowds watched the cartons and sacks of food and drink being docked, the possibility of hunger was the last thing to enter their minds. The thought of becoming a millionaire blocked out everything else.

The only reason Dawson existed at all was its proximity to the gold fields. The climate was atrocious. It was miles from any form of civilization. When the top layer of ground thawed and turned into muck, the mosquitoes rose in black clouds to spread their own brand of misery. One man wrote of the pesky insects.

> They drop into your cup of tea, they . . . fill your spoon before you take it to your lips, you open your mouth . . . and half a dozen mosquitoes sail into your throat. . . .

Those mosquitoes made tough miners so wretched that they sat and sobbed. It was said a few men committed suicide because of them.

IN SPITE of Dawson's rapid growth it was an orderly and well-regulated city. The Mounties kept a firm hand on any potential troublemakers, and there was little thievery or violence. No one was allowed to carry a handgun. Even the gold-laden packtrains were safe, although they were attended by only two muleskinners.

The saloons and dancehalls were closed on Sundays. That fact didn't stop the constantly moving procession of men along the muddy streets. There were sourdoughs, in their fur caps, twill parkas, and mukluks, with their slow, deliberate gait and their clean-shaven faces. These experienced prospectors knew how fast a wet beard freezes in winter. In contrast there were the cheechakos in their rubber or leather boots and their heavy mackinaw coats and their full beards. They walked quickly and nervously and their faces were taut and eager.

Six sternwheelers brought eight hundred tons of food into the Klondike Valley in the summer of 1897, but that wasn't enough to keep up with the rising population. Official notices were posted:

> For those who have not laid in a winter's supply, to remain longer is to court death from starvation, or at least the certainty of sickness from scurvy and other troubles. Starvation now stares everyone in the face who is hoping and waiting for outside relief.

Most people still refused to believe that they couldn't buy food. Didn't they have money and gold? Who ever heard of wealthy men not being able to buy the necessities of life? Determined to buy what they needed, they stood in lines fifty deep in front of the two warehouses. Afraid of violence, the clerks started admitting only one person at a time, locking the door behind him, and doling out his share of the food. Miners with a million dollars in gold dust received no more than the poorest cheechako.

Gold had suddenly become worthless.

People continued to drift in from the White and Chilkoot Passes, while rumbling herds of caribou and great flocks of geese headed in the opposite direction. As the stampeders kept arriving, the unease of the inhabitants of the Klondike slowly turned to panic. Five more steamers laden with food had been expected, but they were now long overdue. Freeze-up had started and with every passing hour the prospect of their making it through to Dawson became dimmer.

One of the officials of the Alaska Commercial Company set off to see whether he could locate the missing steamers. When he spotted them, he knew that the people of the Klondike Valley were in deep trouble. All five ships were stuck in the ice four hundred miles away.

He rushed back to Dawson to warn everyone that there would be no more food until spring. His canoe was spotted coming down the river and soon there were four thousand anxious people waiting on the docks to hear what he had found. The official shouted that they should get out unless they already had enough food to last through the icebound winter months.

"There is no time to lose!" he cried.

For a few moments there was a stunned silence. Then there were screams and hysteria. Mobs threatened to storm the warehouses. Everywhere there was bartering, shouting, begging, and pleading. Restaurants closed as the news spread and miners swarmed in from Eldorado and Bonanza. Within twelve hours fifty boats had pushed off from the docks and three hundred more were preparing to leave. Men who had used all of their wits and resources to get to the gold fields were now using all of their energies to retreat. They formed a great panic-stricken, defeated army.

There was a temporary ray of hope when two of the delayed steamers arrived. They had cached half of their cargoes to lighten their loads and had broken through the ice during a sudden thaw. However, as they passed Circle City their captains had been forced at gunpoint to sell provisions to the one hundred and eighty men there. As a result, what was left for the people of Dawson fell far short of what was needed. It was decided that at least one thousand more people would have to leave the area.

Discouraged stampeders trudged up the gangplanks of the steamers. As they left they were followed by scores of smaller vessels. By now, freeze-up was well under way and the most they could hope for was to get to Fort Yukon or Circle City which were over three hundred miles downriver.

The boats had a constant battle with huge, sharpened cakes of ice which jammed rudders and tore gaping holes in the hulls. Sixty-five miles from Fort Yukon there was a great roaring, grating, rending, and tearing as a mountainous wall of ice closed in the ragged flotilla. Soon the main body of boats was completely imprisoned. Their cold, hungry, and frightened passengers had to walk the rest of the distance.

ALL THAT FALL the exodus continued. By December 1, nine hundred more people were retracing their steps up the frozen river to the passes over five hundred miles away. The jagged, jutting points of ice tore at their clothing and moccasins and shattered their sleds as they crawled and climbed between twenty-foot high barriers of frozen water.

As their strength started failing, they discarded first unnecessary items, then tents, and finally food. Most of them ended up with a meager supply of beans and a single blanket. When they stopped they had no shelter and only a small campfire for warmth.

During this time the temperature rose no higher than fifty below. Anyone moving faster than a snail's pace felt the chill air sear his lungs. Cooked beans burned to pebbles and the lightest touch of bare fingers to metal tore off hunks of skin.

Frostbite resulted in gangrene and hands and feet were amputated. One seventeen-year-old boy lost both legs, but swore that as soon as he was fitted with artificial limbs, he planned to return to stake a claim.

The people who stayed in Dawson slept fitfully on benches in saloons with their jars of gold dust lined up beside them. At the Yukon Hotel, buckskin sacks crammed with nuggets were piled up like cordwood. Their owners slept in hard bunks beneath verminous blankets. A crack in the wall provided ventilation and the only light came from the stubs of candles.

When they woke they dined on beans, stewed apples, bread, and coffee. The meal cost five dollars. To pass the time they gambled away their worthless gold. One man lost nineteen thousand dollars in a day and a half.

Out in the fields the only sound was the creak of the windlasses as the miners continued to work deep in their shafts. The valley floor was dotted with conical heaps of gold-filled gravel which lay black against the snow. The smoke from the thawing fires mingled with the haze of winter. Once in a while a shadowy figure emerged from beneath the ground.

IT WAS to this land that thousands of people were still making their tortuous way over the White Pass. Thousands more were waiting in Skagway for their chance to start the journey. They all believed that when they finally got to Dawson, their troubles would be over.

9

The King of the Bad Men

"Look at my eyes—been snow-blind twice;
*   look where my foot's half gone;*
And that gruesome scar on my left cheek,
*   where the frost-fiend bit to the bone*
Each one a brand of this devil's land,
*   where I've played and I've lost the*
*   game,*
A broken wreck with a craze for 'hooch'
*   and never a cent to my name."*

THE PARSON'S SON—*Service*

WW hile men, women, and children were flee-
ing Dawson that December of 1897, Skagway was
jammed with five thousand stampeders. Businesses
were open twenty-four hours a day. Money-lenders,
saloon keepers, dance-hall girls, packers, and outfitters were making fortunes. Any form of enter-

tainment gained an immediate audience. One man earned money by letting people watch him stuff an unbelievable number of china eggs into his mouth. A trained bear danced in the streets, while its owner passed his hat for donations. An Italian arrived with hundreds of toy balloons and sold them quickly at outrageous prices.

Merchants and entertainers were interested only in making money from the stampeders. The stampeders were interested only in getting to the Klondike. No one had time for civic affairs or for maintaining law and order. Thieves, confidence men, and thugs roamed at will. The only attempt to curb their activities was an occasional lynching when someone was caught stealing from a cache.

Jefferson Randolph Smith, commonly called "Soapy," had arrived in Skagway from Seattle in July, 1897. He immediately took advantage of the chaos to make his fortune. With his slender physique, stylish clothes, and neatly-trimmed Van Dyke beard, he looked like a wealthy southern plantation owner. He was actually an expert con man with a genius for organization.

By midwinter he had bought off the militia, the local police, and the newspaper editor. He had spies stationed in Victoria and Seattle. From the time a prosperous passenger stepped onto the gangplank of a northbound steamer, he was probably being watched. Soapy's men were on the docks, on board ship, and standing on the beach at Skagway. They were on the streets, behind the counters of the outfitters and saloons, in the church pews and along the trails. Every person in the area stood a good chance of losing his money to Soapy by having his pockets picked, by playing in a fixed gambling game, or by being held up at gun point.

Hundreds of people sent telegrams at Soapy's telegraph office. They paid five dollars for every message sent and received. None of them knew that there was no telegraph wire coming into Skagway at that time.

Superintendent Samuel Steele of the Northwest Mounted Police described Skagway as "little better than a hell on earth—about the roughest place in the world." He told of his nights there when the music of the bands in the dance halls was mingled with the shouts of murder, cries for help, and the crackle of gunshots.

All through the winter of 1897–8, Soapy and his men ruled absolutely. His reign stopped only at the summit of the pass. The Mounties had installed Maxim guns there to keep him out of Canada.

WITH the coming of spring, people once more started advancing upon the gold fields. The stampeders who had come over the White and Chilkoot

Passes arrived at Lake Bennett in Canada. They then had to cut lumber and build boats to make the long river trip to Dawson. A tent city arose to house the horde. In April and May the sounds of a thousand rasping saws and five thousand hammers echoed against the foot of the mountains.

On May 29, 1898, the ice broke with a resounding crack. The tents were folded and the city disappeared as if by magic. Within forty-eight hours a flotilla of over seven thousand boats carrying thirty thousand people was making its way toward Dawson.

The Mounties who were stationed near Lake Bennett frowned as they watched them leave. They had done all they could to instruct the newcomers about river safety and had given many of them lessons in boat building. They realized, however, that there were too many inexperienced sailors riding in what could be described as floating coffins. These cheechakos were soon to find that the Yukon River held many dangers—rapids, whirlpools, boulders, sandbars, and great gorges and canyons with jagged rocks.

Dozens of people lost their lives on the treacherous waters. Many more lost their entire outfits. One man had trudged over the Chilkoot with his two thousand pounds of food and gear. His craft was dashed to pieces against a rock when he was halfway down the river to Dawson. He returned to Dyea, restocked his supplies, climbed over the pass once again, and built another boat. This too was wrecked upon a rock.

This final blow was too much to bear. He took out his gun and fired a bullet into his head.

THE WHITE and Chilkoot Passes were not the only route to the gold fields. The "all-water" path from the mouth of the Yukon River to the Klondike was also widely advertised. "Just a pleasant boat trip from St. Michael to Dawson" its promoters said. What they didn't tell their customers about was the brevity of the navigational season in the northland. Eventually, there were twenty-five hundred people on ships which were frozen fast in the ice between Norton Sound, which was on the Bering Sea, and the Klondike.

Out of that number only forty-three ever reached Dawson. The rest eventually made their way back to St. Michael.

Thirty-five hundred people tried the "All-American" route, which started at Valdez on the Gulf of Alaska. From here they walked north over the Valdez glacier, then followed the river system to the Yukon.

The journey over the glacier was a nightmare. The ice rose in a series of benches so high that equipment had to be hauled over them by block and tackle. Travelers suffered the tortures of snow blindness, in which their eyes seemed to be filled with hot sand. They faced blizzards and avalanches and alternate freezing and thawing of the glacial surface. When the weather warmed there was a constant flow of water toward the gulf. Thunderous roars and cracks were heard as great boulders of ice were bounced off canyon walls.

Less than a hundred people who took this route ever arrived in Dawson. Most of the ones who turned back to Valdez were half blind, crippled, or desperately ill from scurvy.

The "All-Canadian" or Ashcroft route started at Vancouver, went north to Ashcroft, then on to Teslin Lake at the headwaters of the Yukon River. Fifteen hundred men and three hundred horses started out this way. They found that the trail was one thousand miles of forests so dense that no light ever came through, even on the rare days when the sun was shining. Poisonous weeds were plentiful, but there was no edible grass for the animals. Clouds of vicious flies and mosquitoes attacked both man and beast as they stumbled through black bogs and over fallen logs and great slippery roots. Rain fell ceaselessly and horses sank up to their bellies in mud and men's legs ached from walking along the gummy roads.

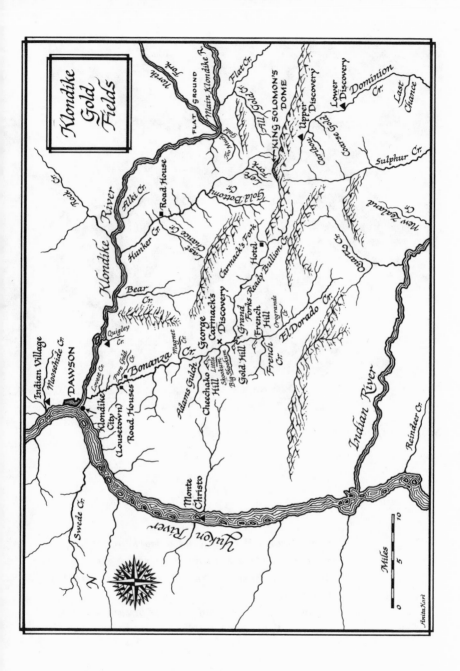

Starting up the White Pass trail to the goldfields.

LEFT: *George Washington Carmack, one of the discoverers of gold in Bonanza Creek.*
RIGHT: *Skookum Jim, another of the discoverers of Bonanza.*
OPPOSITE: *Boxes of gold ready to be shipped from Dawson, September, 1898.*

Stampeders climbing the Chilkoot Pass in the winter of 1897.

Shipping turkeys over the White Pass trail in 1898.

Off to the gold fields by goat team!

Supplies bound for Dawson. Taken at Miles Landing, which is between the lakes at the foot of the passes (Bennett and Linderman) and the Yukon River proper.

A miner's raft entering Lake Bennett from Lake Linderman.

LAKE BENNETT—1898

Boats on Lake Bennett in 1898.

Broadway, Skagway, May, 1898.

Soapy Smith.

Measuring gold dust in a saloon, fall, 1899.

Mounties and stampeders at a border station.

Harriet Pullen in the early 1900s.

Every trail leading into the Klondike Valley had its own brand of misery and frustration. Each one was widely heralded by the men who stood to make money from it—the transportation companies and the merchants who had businesses in the various port cities. A storekeeper in Valdez or St. Michael cared only about selling supplies to eager men who had been enticed to his particular town by widespread, enthusiastic advertising. He didn't care at all that these dearly bought supplies would more than likely be lost in the foaming rapids of the Yukon River or abandoned by a heartbroken adventurer.

DAWSON once more came to life in the spring of 1898 as waves of stampeders swept down the Yukon. Between fifteen thousand and twenty thousand newcomers arrived during that year's navigation season. They bounded from their boats and strode briskly into town. Their voices were loud and excited, their eyes shining with the thrill of being so close to the fulfillment of their dreams.

Where can I start digging? How do I get my share of those five-hundred-dollar pans? Which way do I head to get to the richest claims? Each cheechako cornered every grizzled sourdough he saw and threw questions at him.

He soon heard the discouraging answers and

then joined the throngs of bewildered men who wandered the streets. His voice became quiet. His enthusiastic questioning changed into a timid search for some small bit of evidence that he hadn't come all this way and endured so much hardship for nothing.

Soon most of them stopped even that half-hearted quest. About a third of them left within six weeks of their arrival. So many outfits were being sold that the main street looked like a rummage sale.

The ones who stayed spent their days trudging along the slimy mud-covered walkways or standing in line at the post office, hoping for some word from home. Tons of unsorted mail lay in heaps and there were futile seven hour waits while two Mounties rummaged through the piles.

A few hopeful men spent their time at the Recorder's Office. They kept an eye out for anyone who was registering a claim. Then they followed him to his diggings, pounded in some stakes in the surrounding area, and settled back to see if the miner came up with any good prospects.

As a last resort, desperate men staked claims in Dawson itself. The alert Mounties pulled the stakes up as fast as they were driven into the ground.

The wild dreams of gaining wealth in the

Klondike had been shattered for almost everyone except the people who had been in on the original stampede. However, rumors of new strikes were kept alive by the merchants, who didn't want their customers to leave town. Soon even their enthusiasm wasn't enough to inspire a quickly failing faith. A short time before, Dawson had been called the Golden City, the pot of gold at the end of the rainbow. Many of its disillusioned inhabitants now saw what a terrible trick had been played upon them. There was no gold there. There was only mud, mosquitoes, and a thickening feel of hopelessness in the air.

10

"I Would Do It Over Again."

This is the Law of the Yukon,
that only the Strong shall thrive;
That surely the Weak shall perish,
and only the Fit survive."

THE LAW OF THE YUKON—*Service*

Jostling, shoving, wandering aimlessly in the crowded streets, the newcomers to Dawson started pondering their next move. As they pondered, their despair slowly dissipated. After all, they reasoned, they may have lost the race for the gold, but they *had* tried. They *had* made it to Dawson. That, in itself, was something to brag about.

They could pretend that they were Eldorado kings as they watched Big Alex McDonald, Charley Anderson, and Antone Stander spend their fortunes.

As they followed the millionaires into the saloons and theaters, they took advantage of the free flow of gold. Before long they were like a crowd on a long holiday, and laughter rang out along the streets. Every night Dawson was a huge carnival.

During the day it was a giant marketplace. By the end of August fifty-six steamers had unloaded seventy-four tons of freight at its docks. Mahogany furniture, Persian rugs, cribbage boards, champagne, lobster, opera glasses, and ostrich feathers were offered for sale.

Small shops and open air stands sold bread, ice cream, and fresh fruit. Rifles sold for one dollar. Since the Mounties allowed no one to carry a firearm, the miners cut off the barrels and used them to pipe steam into the frozen earth.

Brooms were one of the few scarce items. When a shipment of them arrived, they were snatched up for seventeen dollars apiece.

Sled dogs, so many of which had been starved and beaten in the race to the Klondike, now became status symbols. Wealthy miners spent thousands of dollars on harness and food for their teams. One man spent over four thousand dollars on bacon alone to feed his six huskies during the winter of 1898–9.

The Klondike kings built hotels, hired butlers to wait on them in their log cabins, and sent to Paris for clothes for their wives.

A miner from Bonanza Creek became angry when his newly arrived nephew expressed dismay at the free spending in Dawson.

"Expense!" the miner cried. "Expense! Don't show your ignorance by using that cheap Outside word. . . . If you have money, spend it; that's what it's for and that's the way we do business."

WHILE the Mounties kept a firm rein on the citizens of Dawson, Soapy Smith still ruled Skagway. He rode at the head of the Fourth of July Day parade in 1898 and shook hands with some of Alaska's highest officials. He had reached the height of his ambition.

During the holiday celebration, however, J. D. Stewart was making his way over the White Pass with twenty-eight hundred dollars in gold dust. He arrived in Skagway on July 7. By the morning of July 8 his money was tucked away in Soapy's safe.

Stewart was not the sort of man to accept the loss quietly. He threatened to tell everyone he met about the robbery. The local merchants knew that hundreds of people with money to spend would soon be leaving Dawson for the Outside. If those stampeders heard about the crime rate in Skagway, they would take alternate routes. The businesses of Skagway would suffer.

Soapy refused to give Stewart his money back.

The merchants and other concerned citizens held a meeting and stationed guards outside of the building to keep Soapy's men away. Frank Reid was one of those guards.

As the day wore on the tension grew. Stores were closed and people stayed behind locked doors, as Soapy threatened revenge on the upstarts who were questioning his rule. Then late in the afternoon, the "King of Skagway" armed himself with three guns and marched toward the meeting house.

Frank Reid confronted him and warned him to stay away. Soapy aimed his rifle, Reid pulled his gun and two shots were fired. Within moments Soapy lay dead and Frank Reid was dying.

When Soapy's gang had been jailed or run out of town, Skagway became a safe place to live for its sixteen hundred permanent residents. People such as Harriet Pullen were at last able to lead honest, industrious lives free from fear. Mrs. Pullen was a widow who had arrived in Skagway with four small sons and seven dollars. She had set up a bakery, cooking pies in pans which she hammered out of old tin cans.

After saving enough money to buy four horses she started freighting gear up the White Pass during the day, while making pies at night. Eventually she became a prominent hotel owner. She never forgot what it was like to be poor, however. She was always eager to help out people who were down on their luck.

There were also heroic women in Dawson. Irish Nellie Cashman ran a boardinghouse and never hesitated to nurse the sick back to health and give the homeless a free room. She became known as the "miner's angel."

Wives worked alongside their husbands in the gold fields. Many single women staked their own claims and mined them alone, often running a bakery or a laundry to provide them with money to live.

Not all men lost their finer human qualities in the hysteria of the stampede. Even among the desperate men on the mountain passes there were some who would stop to help a fallen stranger. One of these came upon an injured man and carried him on his back for the rest of the way. Father William Judge arrived in Dawson with a sled full of medical supplies, after pulling the load in harness with his dog to save the animal's strength. The hospital which he built was constantly full of patients and short of help. He worked from early in the morning until late at night and was awakened from sleep whenever anyone wanted to see him.

He gave his small room to a sick man and slept in the halls. After giving his food and clothing to patients, he came down with pneumonia. When he died in January of 1899, a miner said, "it was as if the whole town had slipped into the river." Everyone who knew the "Saint of Dawson" felt a little better about belonging to the human race.

The Northwest Mounted Police were the quiet heroes of the gold rush. They had an air of dignified authority and seldom had to raise their voices or pull a gun. Surrounded by hysteria, they kept calm. Without the Mounties the entire Klondike Valley could have become another Skagway.

Superintendent Samuel Steele of the Mounties was the only man for whom Soapy Smith had fear and respect. The "Lion of the Yukon" used strength and common sense as he directed his men to maintain order at the summit of the passes, to register boats at Lake Bennett, to police the river and rescue drowning cheechakos, to settle quarrels among partners, and to squelch any hint of criminal activity or violence in Dawson.

Dawson existed as the "San Francisco of the North" from July, 1898, to July, 1899. It boasted dramatic societies, luxurious hotels, schools, and libraries. The gold never stopped circulating in the gambling halls, and people from all over the world came together in its streets.

In April of 1899, the firemen were striking for higher wages and had allowed the fires to go out in the boilers of their engines. When a small fire broke out in a saloon, the fire trucks were useless. The temperature was forty-five below and fires had to be set on the river ice to get to the water supply. The pumps were finally started, but the water froze and burst the hoses before it could reach the nozzles.

Men soaked blankets and threw them over the smaller buildings and dynamited hotels to keep the flames from spreading, but they were defeated from the start. By the time the fire was out over 117 buildings had been destroyed.

Undaunted, the townspeople started rebuilding. As the new buildings went up plate glass replaced canvas windows and the houses had polished wooden floors. The roads were paved and children played on the sidewalks in front of fancy shops.

The sourdoughs grew uneasy when they saw these signs of civilization. When word started filtering into Dawson about the discovery of gold under the sands of Nome, they first started leaving in twos and threes, then in tens and twenties.

Then it was confirmed that a fortune lay under the coastal beaches over which hundreds had passed on their way to the Klondike, and the stampede was on. During a single week in August, eight thousand men left Dawson forever.

THE KLONDIKE gold rush thus ended as quickly as it had started. However, as the years passed it became evident that there would never be another stampede like it. The "Great Stampede of '98" is remembered in story and song, and in all the written memoirs there is no expression of regret.

A man named Walter Curtin had been on a ship which was frozen in the ice of the Yukon River for eight months. He had seen one man die from scurvy and another go mad because of the continual darkness. He himself had suffered from cold and hunger, but thirty years later he looked back upon the experience and wrote the following words:

> I had thirty-five cents in my pocket when I set foot in Alaska. . . . I did not have so much when I left the country more than two years later. . . . I made exactly nothing, but if I could turn the clock back, I would do it over again for less than that.